J 395.4 Min
Minden, Cecilia,
Writing a thank-you letter /
$12.79   on1083465805

W9-AOK-692

3 4028 09953 8028
HARRIS COUNTY PUBLIC LIBRARY

Write It Right

WITHDRAWN

Writing a Thank-You Letter

Thank You

By Cecilia Minden and Kate Roth

Published in the United States of America by
Cherry Lake Publishing
Ann Arbor, Michigan
www.cherrylakepublishing.com

Reading Adviser: Marla Conn MS, Ed., Literacy specialist, Read-Ability, Inc.
Book Designer: Felicia Macheske
Character Illustrator: Carol Herring

Photo Credits: © wavebreakmedia/Shutterstock, 7, 9; © spass/Shutterstock, 13; © ESB Professional/Shutterstock, 15

Graphics Throughout: © simple surface/Shutterstock.com; © Mix3r/Shutterstock.com; © Artefficient/Shutterstock.com; © lemony/Shutterstock.com; © Svetolk/Shutterstock.com; © EV-DA/Shutterstock.com; © briddy/Shutterstock.com; © IreneArt/Shutterstock.com

Copyright © 2020 by Cherry Lake Publishing
All rights reserved. No part of this book may be reproduced or utilized in any
form or by any means without written permission from the publisher.

Library of Congress Cataloging-in-Publication Data has been filed and is available at catalog.loc.gov

Cherry Lake Publishing would like to acknowledge the work of The Partnership for 21st Century Skills.
Please visit *www.p21.org* for more information.

Printed in the United States of America
Corporate Graphics

Table of
CONTENTS

CHAPTER ONE

Why Write a Thank-You Letter?

Did someone do something nice for you? You will want to write a thank-you letter. It tells that person you are thankful for what they did. Think about the last time someone thanked you. Didn't you feel good to hear or read such kind words? A thank-you letter is a great way to let others know that you value them.

This book will help you learn to write two kinds of thank-you letters:

- Thank you for a gift
- Thank you for an **event**

All thank-you letters have five main parts:

1. DATE
(the day, month, and year the letter was written)

2. GREETING
(the words that begin a letter)

3. BODY
(the main part of a letter)

4. CLOSING
(the words that end a letter)

5. SIGNATURE
(the letter writer's name, written by hand)

April 8, 2019

Dear Noah,

Thank you for my terrific birthday gift. I'm very interested in magic. This book will help me work on my skills and come up with new tricks. I'm especially interested in card tricks. Next time I see you, I will show you a new card trick!

Thank you for this wonderful book.

Your friend,
Taylor

You can have a lot of fun designing and writing thank-you letters. They can be written on small, colorful notepaper or cards. The envelope can match the notepaper. Some people like to decorate their card with stickers or drawings.

Here's what you'll need to complete the activities in this book:

- Notebook paper for your **draft**
- Notepaper or cards
- **Envelopes**
- Stamps
- A pencil with an eraser
- A pen

Thank You

Write a personal note even if the card has
"Thank You" printed on the cover.

CHAPTER TWO

Thank You for the Gift!

Think about your gift when you begin to write the thank-you letter. How will you use your gift? Is it something to read, play with, or wear? Is it something you can share with others? Make a list of at least three different things you can say about your gift. This will help you tell the gift giver why you are so thankful for the gift.

Plan your thank-you letter within a few days of getting the gift. That way, your thoughts about it will still be fresh!

ACTIVITY

Make a List

In this activity, you will make a list of what you like about your gift.

INSTRUCTIONS:

1. Write the name of the gift.
2. List a few things you like about the gift.

Sample List

GIFT: a camera from Uncle Mike

- Uncle Mike is a photographer.
- The camera is just the one I wanted.
- He is going to teach me how to take pictures.
- I can learn to take better photos.

CHAPTER THREE

Dear Uncle Mike

Now you have a clear idea about why you like your gift.
Use your list to write a draft of your thank-you letter.

Examples of closings are:
    Love,
    Thank you again,
    You are the best,

Write the Thank-You Letter

In this activity, you will write a thank-you letter for a gift.

INSTRUCTIONS:

1. Start by writing a draft. Write the date at the top of a piece of paper.

2. On the next line, write the greeting "Dear" and the name of the person who gave you the gift.

3. Put a comma after the person's name.

4. **Indent** your first **paragraph**. Begin the body of the letter by writing "Thank you for" and the name of the gift.

5. Use your list about why you liked the gift to write several sentences.

6. End the letter with a closing like "Sincerely" or "Your friend."

7. Put a comma after the closing words.

8. Look over your draft to make sure there are no mistakes. Make sure there is nothing else you want to add.

9. In your best handwriting, copy your draft to the notepaper.

10. Sign your name.

April 23, 2019

Dear Uncle Mike,

    Thank you for the camera. It is just the one I wanted! Thank you also for offering to take me on a photo shoot. I know I can learn a lot from you about how to take pictures.

    I'm really excited about learning to be a photographer like you!

You are the best,
Taylor

In a closing, the first letter of the first word is a capital letter.

You

Check off each step as you write your thank-you.

CHAPTER FOUR

Thank You for Inviting Me!

You should write a thank-you letter after someone takes you to an event. First, make a list of everything you did together at the event. Maybe your friend's mother invited you to join them at a concert. Make a list of why you liked this activity and what made it special. Your friend's family will enjoy remembering what you did together. And your friend's mother will know you were thankful for the fun time.

Music is always a treat!

Make a List

In this activity, you will make a list of things you liked about the event.

INSTRUCTIONS:

1. Write down the name of the event.
2. List a few things you liked about the event.

Sample List

EVENT: concert with friends

- An outdoor concert
- Had a picnic on a blanket
- Everyone asked to sing along
- Great way to spend a fall evening

CHAPTER FIVE

Dear Mrs. Morgan

This thank-you letter looks like the one you wrote for your gift. It has the same five main parts. Use your list to help you remember all the things you want to say. Let the person know you were happy to be invited to such a fun event. Be sure to include something that happened while you were together. This makes your thank-you letter special.

Follow along with the activity instructions on page 11.

A photo of the event is nice to include in your letter.

October 6, 2019

Dear Mrs. Morgan and Sophia,

Thank you for taking me to the concert in the park. It was exciting to go in the evening and see all the lights. I enjoyed having a picnic on a blanket while we listened to the music.

My favorite part was when the band played music so we could all sing along. That was great!

Thank you again,
Taylor

CHAPTER SIX

Signed, Sealed, and Stamped

Now you are ready to mail your thank-you letter. The envelope needs to be addressed. Write clearly so the post office will know where to send the letter.

Your letter is ready to send after you address and stamp the envelope.

Address and Stamp the Envelope

In this activity, you will prepare the envelope.

INSTRUCTIONS:

1. Position the envelope so the **seal flap** is at the top.

2. Be sure to write on the front of the envelope.

3. Write your name and address in the upper left corner.

4. Write the name and address of the person getting the letter in the center of the envelope.

5. Put a stamp in the upper right corner.

Taylor
123 My Street
Anytown, State 10203

Mrs. Morgan and Sophia Morgan
145 Their Street
Anytown, State 10203

Final Check

- Did I start my letter with today's date?
- Did I include a greeting?
- Did I explain why I like the gift or enjoyed the event?
- Did I include a closing and signature?
- Did I include photos if I have any?
- Did I address the envelope correctly?
- Did I remember to put a stamp on the envelope?

Once your final check is complete, you're ready to seal your envelope!

Everyone likes being thanked for their effort!

CHAPTER SEVEN

Other Ways to Say Thank You

It is nice to send a thank-you letter in the mail. Some people may choose to send an email or a text. If you do this, don't just write a quick sentence or two. Be sure you follow the same parts of a thank-you letter.

People do good deeds every day. It is nice to thank them for what they do. Stick a thank-you letter in someone's pocket or locker as a surprise. Maybe you could slip it into their book bag or desk.

Who knows? You may even receive a thank-you letter of your own!

GLOSSARY

draft (DRAFT) a first version of a document, or one that is not final

envelopes (AHN-vuh-lopes) flat paper coverings that are used to mail letters

event (eh-VENT) something of importance that happens

indent (in-DENT) to start a line of writing farther in from the left

edge of a page than the other lines

paragraph (PAIR-uh-graf) a group of sentences about a certain idea or subject

seal flap (SEEL FLAP) the part of an envelope that folds down to close it

BOOKS

Marsico, Katie. *Please and Thank You!*. Ann Arbor, MI: Cherry Lake Publishing, 2013.

Summers, Jean. *The Kids' Guide to Writing Great Thank-You Notes*. Cranston, RI: Writers Collective, 2006.

WEBSITE

KidsPrintables.com
www.kidprintables.com/thankyounotes
Use these fun designs to create your thank-you notes.

Harris County Public Library
Houston, Texas

INDEX

About the AUTHORS

Cecilia Minden is the former director of the Language and Literacy Program at Harvard Graduate School of Education. She earned her doctorate from the University of Virginia. Her research focused on early literacy skills. She is currently a literacy consultant and the author of over 100 books for children. Dr. Minden lives with her family in McKinney, Texas. She loves to spend time reading books and writing to family and friends.

Kate Roth has a doctorate from Harvard University in language and literacy and a master's degree from Columbia University Teachers College in curriculum and teaching. Her work focuses on writing instruction in the primary grades. She has taught kindergarten, first grade, and Reading Recovery. She has also instructed hundreds of teachers from around the world in early literacy prac  She lived with her husband and three children in China for many years, and now they live in Co   icut.